HOW TO DISCIPLINE CHILDREN WITHOUT FEELING GUILTY

EN71030

by
Harris Clemes, Ph.D.
Reynold Bean, Ed.M.

Edited by
Janet Gluckman

ENRICH
From
Price/Stern/Sloan
Publishers, Inc.

presents **THE WHOLE CHILD SERIES**

1980 revised edition - Sixth Printing 1985
Copyright © 1978 Reynold Bean, Harris Clemes
Published by Price/Stern/Sloan Publishers, Inc.
410 N. La Cienega Blvd., Los Angeles, California 90048
All Rights Reserved Under International Convention
Printed IN U.S.A.
ISBN 0-933358-77-6

CONTENTS

INTRODUCTION

Do the following complaints remind you of your child?

"Johnnie doesn't listen to me when I tell him to do something."

"It's a continual struggle to get Sara to bed at a reasonable hour."

"Ronnie continues to lie, even when he's confronted with the obvious truth."

"Is it reasonable for an eight-year-old to continually wet his bed?"

"Alex's teachers are simply fed up with him. He doesn't do any work and is always making trouble."

"Jane always complains of stomach aches, and doesn't want to go to school."

A child with those chronic behavior problems does not necessarily have a deep-seated emotional problem. Children more often become "problems" because of the malfunctioning of the social systems in which they live. Their behavior is a response to the way their environment handles them, overall.

The number of children who actually have severe emotional problems is very small, so small, that most parents can safely assume that their child doesn't. In instances where a serious psychological problem is present, the behavior of the child is so bizarre and strange that it is usually clear that something serious is wrong.

All children are different. Just because several children grow up in the same family is no guarantee that they will behave similarly. No one's life experience is like anyone else's. This is the basis of our individuality. Nor are they born knowing how to act the way their parents want them to. This has to be learned—taught to them by parents who are not necessarily expert teachers.

The systems of surmounting importance in a child's life are, first, his* family, and second, his school.

*He, rather than he or she, is used in the text for the sake of fluidity.

This handbook is designed to help parents and others who work with children create a well functioning family system in which a child can grow. Although the approach was designed primarily for use by parents, it can readily be adapted for use in the classroom. Teachers will benefit by familiarity with the system because it will enable them to provide continuity for the child who is being guided by its rules and limits. More than that, the teacher can be instrumental in letting parents know that this handbook exists by making copies available to them.

This book is based on certain beliefs about the relationship between parents and children, and is directed toward parents who believe similarly, but are having problems "making it happen."

Among these beliefs are:

- Parents and children are not equals in all matters. The child's natural dependence on parents for security, support, and nurturing, gives parents a natural responsibility and authority in broad areas of a child's life.

- Parents who punish children for misbehavior are not "bad" parents. Punishment is only bad if (1) it is ineffective in changing the way a child acts, or (2) it produces unintended bad consequences for the child. Realistic punishment doesn't have to do either one.

- Parents promote secure feelings in children when they mean what they say, are clear about what they mean, and are consistent and predictable in what they do.

- Responsibility can only be learned by children when they are being held accountable for their behavior. Any realistic system of accountability must have consequences in it.

- One of the most important things that children need to be taught is how to be responsible for their own behavior. This sense of responsibility can and should be taught to them by parents.

- Parental authority does not have to be exercised in ways that are abusive, mean, insensitive, or damaging to a child, but authority *must* rest with the parents.

• Most problems between parents and children result from a struggle for power and control. Parents must know how to win in this struggle when necessary, so that they can give power to children when advisable.

The list of problems which parents bring to counselors is never-ending. Below is a partial list of the kinds of things which parents are concerned about:

Bedwetting	Poor school attendance
Lack of attention	Cutting classes
Fighting with siblings	Setting fires
Talking back	Won't do chores
Lying	Irresponsible behavior
Bedtime fights	Arguing continually
Sleeping with parents	Hitting parents
Crying inappropriately	Constantly pouting
Stealing	Running away
Won't come home on time	Destroying property

Despite the fact that all children are different, many—if not most—of them have the above problems in common. Parents can successfully set limits and rules for their children, i.e. discipline them in such a manner that they succeed in resolving chronic behavioral problems.

—The Authors

I.
A Process

Setting rules, establishing consequences for breaking rules, and using consistent discipline are the keynotes to resolving most of the problems parents have with children.

Effective rules help a child feel secure so that he does not have to misbehave. This process allows parents to maintain effective authority in the home, and establishes a proper relationship between parents and children.

A body of rules defines relationships among members of a family, offers a basis for decision making, and provides a model for the manner in which change should occur in the family. It allows people to know "where things are at," and to determine where they *ought* to be.

The process of setting rules and limits for children is not something that is done once-and-for-all. Every so often, it is necessary to change the rules and limits within which a child lives, in order to provide for changing circumstances, physical growth, aging, and new conditions in the family's life.

Without such a process in the family, chaos is unavoidable. When there is lack of understanding, confusion as to roles and appropriate behavior, a great deal of insecurity and anxiety will arise in all members of the family.

II.
Making Decisions About Your Children

Many parents have difficulty in knowing how to act with their children because they feel they must have some mysterious knowledge which is only possessed by a small band of very wise specialists who "really" know what is right to do with children. One could accuse the authors of this manual of reinforcing this silliness, but it is hoped that the information contained in this manual is straight-forward and practical enough to make sense to the average parent.

Most parents are not child psychologists. Besides, doctors, educators, and psychologists sometimes have children with problems, too. Given the enormous amount of material that is published and printed about raising children by eminent psychologists, educators, doctors, etc., some parents feel that it may be necessary to have a doctorate in some medical field in order to be an adequate parent. Since this is clearly not possible, parents really have to make do with the wisdom and knowledge they have accumulated from their own life experience and that of others with whom they can share.

This burden of not being confident about what to do is what makes it hard for so many parents to make decisions about how to handle their children. It has been our experience that many parents who possess adequate resources are still somewhat confused, indecisive, and guilt-ridden when it comes to outlining a program of child management that is comfortable for them. This problem results in two patterns of parental behavior, both of which lead nowhere. One is that the parent will do nothing, other than to react on the basis of impulse and emotion. The other is that parents will continue to try new things all the time, not really giving any one procedure a long enough trial before shifting to something else. This makes evaluation of results very difficult. For some parents, any outcome less than immediate spontaneous insight and answers to problems is a sign of personal inadequacy. This is sheer foolishness. No one was born into this world being a parent. Being a parent is something that must be learned, and it is clear that most of us learn best by doing. There are many problems which parents cannot learn to solve until they face them head-on with their children. At such times, the answers to such problems are not often immediately clear. Parents have to give thought, analysis, and contemplation to many problems and use good planning in order to solve them.

Making decisions about what to do with our children is no easy matter. We, as parents, are continually haunted by the possibility that some decision we make will lead to bad ends for us and for our children in the future. We cannot read the future, nor do we have a crystal ball regarding the consequences of our actions. *Simply stated, we have to do the best we can with what we've got.* If we are burdened with feelings of inadequacy or guilt, we, of course, will reach the conclusion that "we ain't got enuff."

As a parent, you need to find the time to sit down, analyze your children's problems and plan what to do. Later on in this handbook, you will be shown what steps to take in analyzing the problems.

When parents are indecisive regarding their children, the children sense it, and it affects their feelings of security and well-being. In the long run, it is probably better for parents to act decisively than to worry too much about always making the right decision. If we make a poor decision, we and our children are still attached to each other, and we can correct mistakes made in the past. It is this willingness to act decisively, even in the light of making mistakes, that enables parents to have some degree of confidence that they do have the capability to correct mistakes.

Parents who are *indecisive* provide an opportunity for children who are manipulative, as most of them are at one time or another, to work on the parents and create even greater stress. When parents are *decisive*, the child learns that the parents mean what they say, are willing to follow through, and are not capable of being manipulated. When parents are willing to admit mistakes and learn from them, they create a climate for children to be willing to admit mistakes and learn from theirs.

III.
Undisciplined Parents Will Have Undisciplined Children

Disciplined parents, that is, those who are consistent, reasonable, and communicate directly and clearly, can create a system and be models for children. That will encourage the child to become self-disciplined. *The chief reason that children who are problems don't change, is that their parents don't change in the way they handle the problems.*

Many parents try to force their children to act appropriately without really considering the cause or nature of the behavior that they're attempting to change. Most people learn about being parents by reference to the models they saw in their own upbringing. What they learned was from the perspective of a child. Their perspective as parents is different, and it's hard making the shift. Parents who see the need for change may feel that they are admitting they've been mistaken in the way they handled the problem previously.

Basing the way we handle our children on what *we* experienced as children has inherent dangers. The chief one rests on the fact that our children are different from us, just as we are different from our parents. While it is true that we have many *similarities* to our parents, just as our children have many similarities to us, it is the *differences* that are important. Sometimes, the way we model our own parental behavior is also affected by the reactions that we had to that behavior. In other words, there were things that our parents did to us that we didn't like. Sometimes, instead of really understanding our reactions to our parents, we simply do the same things to our

13

children, often because we don't know what else to do. You might try to think about how your parents handled you in various situations and determine whether you feel it was appropriate to you as a child. If it was, use the technique, because it may work for your children. If it was not, then be ready to change from the way your parents handled you so that you can create a better situation with your own children.

The need to justify one's behavior, thus placing the problem in or on the child, is one of the chief blocks to parents acting appropriately with their children. Parents who are unwilling to see *themselves* as the source of the problem are inclined to believe that their children have deep-seated psychological or emotional disorders, and come to a counselor or therapist in hopes that this belief will be confirmed. In reality, most children's misbehavior does *not* imply emotional disorder, but rather is an attempt by the child to deal in the best way he knows how with the situation maintained by his parent.

Some parental resistance is simply a consequence of inertia. This means that the parents' usual way of reacting is so much a habit that any suggestion to change fails because of the common human tendency to maintain old habits.

Most parents maintain old habits not because of bad will, but rather out of laziness, and lack of self-discipline. Many parents plead that they have tried everything possible to change a child's behavior. What they don't realize is that the *way* they have tried things (not the things they have tried) has not worked.

Most children's problems involve some game that they are playing with their parents. The child has manipulated and controlled the parents' responses in certain ways. Many parents feel that looking at the problem in this way puts them and the child in a bad light, and thus they resist. This manual proposes a method which can help parents deal with a child's manipulation.

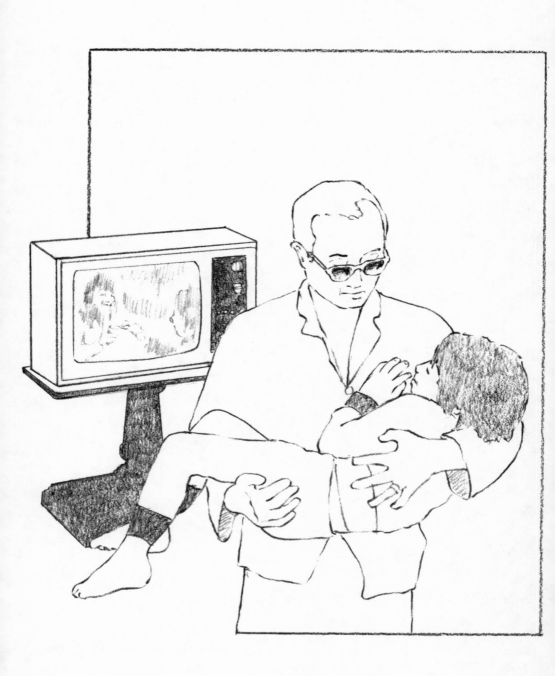

IV.
Games Between Parents and Children

There is a standard relationship that occurs between parents and children, in cases where the child is said to have a problem. The *Basic Game* goes something like this: The child commits an offense, or performs an act, that he knows the parent does not approve of. The parent reacts strongly, and if it's a continuing pattern, overreacts and either hits or yells at the child. The child will then cry, pout, accuse the parents of being bad, or attempt to make the parent feel guilty for his or her overreactive behavior. The parent, sooner or later, *will* begin to feel guilty for what was done and will try to make up to the child in some way, through a reward, by not responding so severely the next time the child acts that way, or not responding at all—thus giving up. The child turns out to be the winner in this game, since he has been able to get the parent to feel guilty, and to do something nice for him, or retreat from the field of battle.

That is the Basic Game—there are many versions of it that occur in every family. But when the particular issues and variations are pushed aside, the continuing reaction, overreaction, guilt, and remorse of the parent usually wind up increasing the inappropriate behavior of a particular child.

Many parents really feel bad when their children say such things as: "I hate you," "You're a bad parent," "I want to go away from home," "You don't understand me," "I don't like you." These are some of the best tools the child has for manipulating and controlling the parents. The parent, on the other hand, frequently and without being aware of it, rewards the inappropriate behavior of the child through giving gifts, like bribes, or too much sympathy. For example, the mother of a bedwetting child may feel guilty about forcing the child to control his bedwetting. She tries to be more protective and understanding. The behavior of the mother is something that the child wants and needs; if bedwetting can get this response, the child is likely to continue to do it.

When children resist the bedtime imposed upon them by their parents by asking for drinks of water, going to the bathroom, asking for crackers because they're hungry, parents respond by trying to be especially nice to the child in order to get him to sleep. The parents' behavior unfortunately encourages the child to stay up later.

Similarly, parents demand responsibility from their children in doing chores, and will pressure them into doing them. The children will resist. If they continue to resist, the parent will either become guilty by their overreaction to what on the surface appears to be a small infraction, or will throw up their hands in defeat and say, "It's easier for me to do it myself, anyway," thus allowing the child to avoid fulfilling the responsibility.

The above descriptions are just some of the games that go on between parents and children. The end result of most of these games is that the parent is controlled by the child.

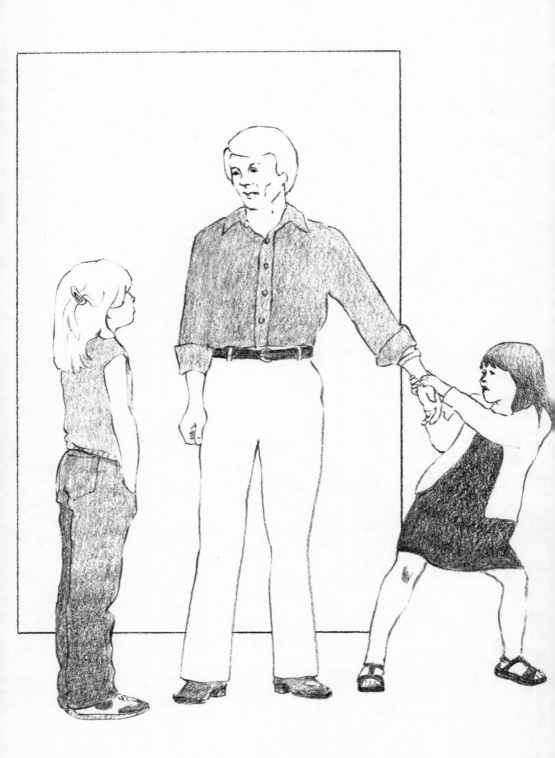

V.
How Parents Are Controlled by Children

It seems that many children are gamblers. They play the odds relative to how much they can get away with. Most children are willing to accept a 50/50 break—in other words, getting away with something 50% of the time. Those aren't bad odds, especially if the act in question is sufficiently important and rewarding for the child to take the risk.

Fundamentally, there are two ways in which children control parents. The first is to make the parent do what the child wants done. The second is to make the parent do something that the parent does not want to do. Many parents are more successful in avoiding the former kind of control than they are the latter. Most parents are not very successful in avoiding the second kind of control.

There are some obvious ways in which children force the parent to do what the child wants. The most natural and obvious ones are such things as crying to get his own way, whining, pouting, and doing other things which stimulate guilt and make the parent back down or change the rules. Some children lean on the parent for so long that the parent will give in to the pressure and simply do what the child wants. For example, one woman, convinced by her child that he had "leg spasms," drove him wherever he had to go. The mother was, of course, quite annoyed and frustrated by this, but felt that the medical problem was most important. (It should be noted that the child had been to doctors who could find no physical problem.) This child had a bicycle but didn't like to ride it very far from home. When the mother finally imposed a limit on taking the child to and from places, and made the child ride his bicycle, the leg spasms ceased.

One of the most effective ways children control parents is by dragging their feet when doing chores. *These children rarely don't do the chore:* They simply take so long doing it, or do it so poorly, that the parent decides that it's easier and more efficient to do the chore himself. Thus the child is excused from the responsibility.

Some children seem to like to toy with their parents. They know all the buttons to push to make the parents react with anger or resentment. More than that, they know that sooner or later the parent will feel guilty and respond by doing something for them to make the child act nicely toward the parent. But children don't always care if they get any benefit in return. In most cases, they are simply exercising their capacity to get the parent angry as an expression of their growing sense of control.

Parents become extremely frustrated, resentful, angry and guilty when it comes to the second form of control that the child has over them, that is: getting the parent to do something that the parent does not want to do. Yet it is a trap parents fall into very easily. Most parents do not *want* to hit their children or have to ground the children and live with them for a week hanging around the house. Worse still, those actions on the part of parents rarely seem to bring about changes in the child's behavior for any significant period of time. Instead, the usual result is that the parents feel guilty, give up, and do not discipline the child consistently.

VI.
Parental Agreement and Disagreement

It is generally believed that problems with a child are often caused by parents disagreeing with each other about how to handle the child. *What is overlooked is that often the cause of those disagreements between parents is the child's behavior.*

Often when parents disagree about what to do about a child's behavior, one becomes the "good parent" and the other becomes the "bad parent." One, more often than not, allows the child to do what he wants; the other, more often than not, does not permit the child to do what he wants. One parent will take the child's side in arguments; the other parent is like an outsider to the partnership between the "good parent" and the child. Often the child, without parents' awareness, is manipulating the parents to disagree. Parents tend to believe the myth that they are in control, when in many cases the child is.

It is true that disagreements about how to raise children is only one of the disagreements that may exist within a marriage. Where disagreement does exist, the child, for obvious reasons, may intensify this disagreement in order to gain his own ends. Many children play one parent off against the other. By doing this, they create more dissension between the marital partners. This does not mean the child is "bad;" he or she is simply trying to get things going his or her way. Many parents and counselors find the above model hard to accept, insofar as they are committed to the myth that parents are in control of the family.

When parents disagree about how to handle children, they are not in control. Under such conditions, the child has too much power for making decisions and manipulating the behavior of the parents. This power isn't good for the child because it promotes an unrealistic sense of authority. It also produces anxiety because the child feels out of control. If the child has no good way to deal with this anxiety, it will show up as deviant behavior.

The basis for effective rule setting is agreement between parents. This does not mean that parents have to agree about everything. Such a goal is unrealistic. But parents must at least agree on those rules that they choose to set. The process for reaching agreement about these rules is simply sitting down, talking about the problem areas, and reaching agreement upon the rules and the consequences. Most, if not all, parents are capable of doing at least this much, even if they have disagreements on other issues. We have seen in our practice that when this is done, it frequently provides a basis for parents sitting down and discussing other issues.

VII.
Punishment

The word "punishment," like so many others in our language, means something different now than it did ten or twenty years ago. To some people, punishment has become essentially a dirty word. We try to avoid the word in our continuing attempts to get away from a past in which punishment was often harsh and seen as necessary to eliminate evil. We have tended to not only avoid the word itself, but also to avoid doing the things necessary to establish limits. For this reason we may not wish to talk about "punishment." But we may, on the other hand, wish to establish "consequences" for certain kinds of behavior.

Having consequences imposed on us for our behavior is no more than the simple reality with which we live. As adults, we are usually rewarded or punished on the basis of our performance. Our performance on the job will lead to promotion and raise in salary, or to reprimand and firing. *Learning that there are consequences for what we do is an aid to developing a sense of reality.*

In a family, there needs to be a balance between reward and punishment. If only reward or only punishment is used, then the child will not learn what is necessary for him to learn.

Being willing to look at the issue of punishment is sometimes difficult for parents. But if a rule is to be effective, then consequences must result from breaking it, or else the rule itself has little meaning. It should be remembered that being *consistent* in applying the consequences is more effective than being *severe*.

VIII.
Steps in Establishing Rules and Limits

The steps to take in setting up rules are:

A. Carefully observe your child.

B. Analyze the problem.

C. Set up the rules.

D. Be consistent in applying the rules.

How to Observe Your Children at Home

Strange as it may sound, one of the reasons that parents have a hard time managing the behavior of their children is that they really do not know them. What we mean by this is that parents tend to see their children only in relationship to themselves. This is especially true with very young children. Parents rarely have the opportunity to see their child when he is unaware of their presence. The very presence of a parent can influence the child's behavior in a variety of ways. Thus, the parents may believe that what they see is the actual behavior, or true nature of their own child, when in fact, it is that part of their child's behavior which is being influenced by the parent being present. This is especially true when a child has some behavior problem.

Very often, children control what it is they wish the parents to see. They will cry to distract their parents from seeing something they have done wrong; they will argue or talk back in order to get parents to argue about one thing rather than something else that the child would rather avoid. Most of us are creatures of habit, and will tend to see what we expect to see. Many children quickly learn what parents expect to see and act accordingly, especially if they get attention or are rewarded for it. We tend to see our children as being extensions of our own personalities and often do not see those things which would show the child as being unique and different from us. It is for these reasons that we need to be cautious about making quick judgments about the meaning of our children's behavior without having observed them at some length and in a variety of situations.

Parents frequently hear something about their child's behavior in other situations which amazes them, since *they* have never seen this behavior in their own child. In order to understand that behavior and have some sense of how their influence is affecting the child, parents have to be able to observe without the child being aware of their presence.

This is difficult but not impossible. It requires taking a bit of time and thinking carefully about what you are doing. For example, when your child is in the back yard playing, it is possible to stand by a window and watch the child for a few minutes. When your child is taking a bath, it is possible to stand at the bathroom door and watch unobserved. When you're out with a group of friends or family, where there are a number of children present, you can watch your child in relationship with other children.

Another way of getting some feedback is to ask friends or relatives to tell you what they see about your child's behavior, even when you are around. It is sometimes difficult to see the forest for the trees, and an objective observer who is not deeply involved with your child may have some observations which would be helpful to you.

Something to avoid when observing a child is the tendency to see only the things that he is doing wrong, rather than observing all of the behavior that is actually there.

One of the difficulties many parents experience with observing is the desire to interfere in the child's behavior. Remember, you may want your children to "act right," but inappropriate intervention frequently only creates misbehavior in the child. Parents should exercise caution when they are observing the child. If he is doing something they don't approve of, but which will not lead to serious or bad ends, the parents should discipline themselves not to intervene at that time. This is especially important because a child so easily develops a sensitivity to being observed by the parent and that makes it more difficult to perform those kinds of observations in the future.

There are parents who are unaware of how difficult their children actually are, and cannot understand why their children seem to be picked on, criticized, and have a bad reputation with other children. If the parents, in these cases, were to take the opportunity to observe their child, they might very well find out why.

On the other hand, many parents have reported to us that when they observe their child in this way, they are surprised to find that the child's behavior is frequently better than they thought it would be. Some have seen their child solving problems with other children, when in the past all they have been aware of is their child coming to them for solutions. Other parents have reported witnessing their child being helpful or caring toward others when they have only noticed self-centered or self-indulgent behavior in the past.

When attempting to set up rules and consequences it is helpful for parents to find *frequent* opportunities for observing their children. Frequent observations will give the parent a more well-rounded view of the child's abilities and behavior. Observing children is very much like detective work. You should be looking for clues which can be used to develop the good behavior that you are trying to bring about so that you can teach your child to act correctly in lots of different situations.

How to Analyze a Problem

First of all, *identify the problem.* In many instances, the only way to define a problem is by attempting a trial-and-error solution. If the solution works, the definition of the problem was more than likely correct. If it doesn't, one can at least have some confidence that such a definition was incorrect, thus reducing the alternatives.

The best way to define a problem is to identify a behavior which you want to change. As an example, take the child who is talking back to parents. The problem is not to get the child to stop *wanting* to talk back; the problem is to *stop* the child from talking back. One of the usual mistakes that parents make is to define a problem so as to try to change the child's feelings or emotional states. The more effective approach is to work at changing the child's actual behavior.

35

If parents can change behavior, more often than not the emotional state that prompted the behavior will also change. Parents find themselves frustrated by not being able to change their child's "attitude." Attitude is a reaction to a set of circumstances; when circumstances change, attitudes usually change, too. When we are disturbed about the way our children act, we should continue to look at behavior as the problem, rather than feelings or emotional states. When we can understand what we want to do in terms of specific behavior that we want to change, then the job of setting rules to change this behavior is much simplified.

Once the problem has some definition to it, the next stage is to *analyze* the problem. To do that, you need as much information about it as possible: When did the problem arise? How did it arise? What are the consequences of the problem? What is your involvement? How do you react? Do you understand why you react that way? What would you like to be able to do? How would you like to have this situation resolve itself? In order to analyze the problem, it is best for the parent or parents to be able to talk the situation over with each other or with someone else. Most people seem to profit from sharing their problems with others, so that they can have some reflection and feedback about the way they are going about analyzing it. You should not look for simple answers from other people; they may not know enough about the situation to provide solutions. But at least they may be able to help you to refine your understanding of the problem.

After you analyze the problem, the next step is to *consider the various alternatives* you have for solving it. Too often, we grab at any straw and adopt the first likely solution to a problem. If we can control our impulse to do this, and try to think of a number of alternatives, we might find one that fits better. Parents should not jump too quickly to a solution. If the problem has been a long-standing one, meaning you've had it for some time, it is best to give yourself some time to come up with a solution. Rome wasn't built in a day.

After parents have thought of a number of different alternatives, it is important to look at each of them in the light of *your capability* to do what is necessary, the *likely consequences* this might have on you and your child, and *whether the solution is reasonable* with reference to time, energy, and money. When you have looked at the alternatives from this point of view, it becomes much easier to select one of them. Once this selection is made, it is important to take time to plan for action.

How to Set a Rule

What do we mean by a rule? A rule is:

- A *statement* by which a child can know what is expected of him.

- A *description* which enables a child to determine how and when a thing should be done.

- A *definition* which gives the child the opportunity to judge right from wrong, correct from incorrect, and appropriate from inappropriate.

- A *communication* which allows the child to know what is expected of him, what the parents' values are, and what the parents define as good behavior. In turn, a rule allows the parents to know when the child has acted inappropriately, or when necessary tasks have been performed.

- A *method* of organizing the life of a family within a household. It allows people to know what their own and others' responsibilities are. It allows definitions in timing and in roles.

- A *device* for reducing tension by making things clear and allowing all parties to know with some predictability what events are to occur, and when. Furthermore, rules enable parents to teach their children about order, responsibility, values, attitudes, and all those things which are necessary for a child to learn in the home, before he begins to learn about them in the world.

The following description of how to set up a rule fits for all rules, whether one or more is set up at a time. This process may also be used as follow-up, when the parents and/or child feel that the rule should be changed.

The most critical beginning for rule-setting is for the parents to sit down with each other, discuss the problems that the children present, and decide on those areas for which rules must be created. In single-parent families it's important that the parent talk to a friend, relative, or counselor about the ideas and get their reactions.

When thinking about rules, parents should be aware that they will be dealing with a specific and concrete behavior of the child. Rules that are designed to change *attitudes* will not be effective rules. Parents have no direct control over what goes on in the child's mind or feelings. Parents do have control over what the child does. Thus all rules should be designed in terms of specific actions that are required from the child.

What are the characteristics of a rule that works?

Rules must be reasonable. By reasonable we mean that a) there are resources available for the child to carry out the rule effectively; b) sufficient time is allowed for the child to do it—this does not mean that endless time is allowed, but if a task must be done by a certain time, then that time must be reasonable in light of family functions and the child's other needs and activities; c) the child must be able to carry out the rules effectively. If a very short child is expected to do some chore which involves working around high places, the parent must know that the child has the ability to climb a ladder, or the rule may not be reasonable. For very small children, very heavy work would usually be unreasonable.

Parents must be sure that they can tell when the rule has been obeyed or when it has been broken. Rules that try to control things that the parent cannot easily check do not work The parent should be able to know whether or not the rule has been met by looking at the clock, or by checking the results of the activity.

The rule must be described in detail. The rule must be described in enough detail so that both the child and the parent know whether or not the rule has been fulfilled. Thus, a rule which just states, "the garbage must be taken out," is not a good rule. What must be determined is exactly how the garbage must be taken out, i.e. the conditions under which the parent will be satisfied with the operation. It is not permissible to have garbage left around the kitchen or under the sink. The top must be replaced on the garbage can. Fresh garbage bags must be placed in the container, and the container must be returned to its usual place. The rule must define and describe what is necessary to carry it out—dotting the i's and crossing the t's.

A time limit should be set for rules. Time limits are such things as: "Before you go to school," "By four o'clock," "Immediately after supper," etc. Rules which do not have time limits give rise to arguments about when the chore will be done or rule followed. Rules about specific behavior may be stated like this: "If I find that you're doing thus and so, I will warn you and you will have five minutes to stop, or else some consequence will occur."

Time limits for rules are necessary and important. Time limits help to establish whether a rule has been obeyed. All rules should have time limits on them. Time limits help to promote order and reduce disagreement, anxiety, and guilt. They provide predictability for both parents and child. Predictability is necessary for family living in order to avoid excessive chaos and confusion. The best time limit to use is defined by the clock. The next best way is to use a time limit which is determined by regular activities, i.e. after supper, before leaving for school, etc. The poorest kind of time limit is one which is determined by an activity which itself can vary in time—after you come in from play, before you watch television, etc.

There should be consequences which occur if the rule is broken. Use consequences which are important to the child. A consequence which may appear to be a punishment to the parent is not necessarily one to the child. Suggestions: For children who like to watch TV, not being able to watch it is a punishment. For children who never watch TV, taking television away from them is not a punishment. Children who don't like dessert will not feel punished if they are not allowed to eat it. Thus, the parents must look at the child's values and interests so as to determine which ones can be used as a form of punishment.

Punishments or consequences must be reasonable from the parents' point of view, too. *Punishments that are too severe, which create guilt or excessive concern in the parent, are not good punishments.* One criterion for punishment is that the parent should be willing to do it without guilt. Parents can determine this for themselves, and should also find punishments which do not take too much of the parents' time or energy. "Grounding" a child for a long time keeps the child in the house for days on end. That generally means the parent will continually be "bugged" and is, therefore, not a good consequence.

Consequences should occur as soon as possible, and should, when possible, be on the day that the infraction has been committed. Consequences must be applied consistently. For this reason, parents should set up consequences which they can do easily. Punishments which require the parents to do special tasks, or to spend a lot of time watching the child, are ones which are not applied consistently. The general rule is that *consistency is more effective than severity.*

After parents have decided on the rules and consequences, *the next step is to call a family council;* at this time, if possible, both parents and all of the children to whom the rules apply should be present. The first job of the parents is to lay out the problem as they see it. They may ask for feedback from the children to find out how they see the problem, but this is not absolutely required. But as the child gets older, it would be important that he have more of a voice in the setting of the rules and analyzing the problem.

Some explanations should be given as to why the rules need to be established. Along with this, it is very good for the parents to explain that in the past they have not been able to cope with the problem very well, and now have decided to do something which will deal with the problem effectively.

After laying out the problem, the parents should explain the rules that have been defined, the time limits, and the consequences which will occur if the rules are broken. It is very important that the child completely understand what the rules and consequences are. Regarding the time limit, the child should be able to tell time or have some way to find out what the time is. The parent should explain the rules in language which the child can understand. One of the simplest ways to insure that the child understands the rule, and thus has no excuse for saying he didn't understand, is to ask that he repeat all aspects of the rules which have been explained. Once the child has done this, the parents can be assured that the child has heard the rule. In addition, parents should make a list of rules, time limits, and consequences. One copy should be posted in the child's room; the other should be kept by the parent.

During this process, the child may attempt to resist the rule. After all, the rule will tend to stop the child from playing the game that surrounds this particular behavior. Children may resist in a number of ways. They may start crying. They may accuse the parent of being mean and overbearing. They may say that irrespective of what the parent does to them, they will not follow the rule. Various approaches may be used by the child as a way to get the parent to back down. The parents must see the game which is being played. The child's resistance is another attempt to control the parents by making them do something that they don't want to do. The parents' goal is to be firm with the rule. If the child can make the parent back off, then the child has won. While the child may be resisting, the parents should pay attention to what he says. This attention can be paid by recognizing the child's feelings and saying "I understand that you don't want this to happen," or, "I'm sorry that it makes you feel so bad." The parent should not accept the challenge to the rule setting procedure, unless the child has an alternative which deals as well with the problem as the parents' rules. If the child does not have a better alternative, then the parents may recognize the child's feelings, but their purpose should not be compromised by the outburst.

A further aspect of rule setting is a simple one. It is that *the rule should become effective on the day following this family conference.*

The last and most critical aspect of rule setting is that *the parent should follow through.* On the day following the conference, the parent should be especially aware of the child's behavior. There should be no deviation from the rule as stated on the previous day. The parent should not repeat the rule to the child at any time during the day, unless the child *asks* for reaffirmation of the rule. If the time limit is broken, e.g. if the garbage is to be taken out by five o'clock and the clock says two minutes after five, the parent should make sure that the child does the chore, as well as informing him that the punishment which was associated with it is going to be imposed directly. There should be no excuses possible. The child must begin to take responsibility for the task. *If the parent reminds him, the parent has taken the responsibility.* The parents must expect the child to remember what to do, when to do it, and how to do it; no reminders should be given to the child. At this point, self-discipline on the part of the parent is very important. The parents should have talked about this beforehand, be ready to support each other, or be able to act independently of each other, if necessary.

The Importance of Being Consistent

Consistency is a way of letting the child know that the parents mean what they say. Consistent application of a rule and a mild punishment will have more effect in the long run on a child, than inconsistency and severe punishment. Consistency is a way for the parents to show the child that they are aware of his behavior. By knowing that the parents are aware of his behavior, a child has added encouragement to act appropriately.

By being consistent, parents help children, particularly younger children, to feel secure. When parents are inconsistent, their children become anxious because they cannot predict what their parents will do. It almost seems that children misbehave not only because of their anxiety, but as a way to get the parent to set limits.

Attempting to consistently apply a bad rule will result in resentment and angry attacks by both the child and the parent. Inconsistent application of a good rule will result in the child's behavior not being controlled by the parent. Consistent application of good rules will promote order and discipline in the family, allow for security, and promote good will. Most parents are less consistent than they should be, but think they're more consistent than they are. When parents don't have a clear and regular system of rules, they really don't have anything to be consistent about. Having such a system can aid parents to be consistent.

IX.
Some Examples
of Rules

When establishing rules, the parent should set up a sheet with the rules, time limits, and punishments listed on it. One copy of this should be pinned up in the child's room as a continuing reminder. The parent should keep the other copy in case the child "inadvertently" loses the paper.

The following are a few examples of rules. They are only suggestions for parents, and should be changed to fit individual situations:

Taking out the garbage. The garbage basket should be taken from under the sink in the kitchen. It should be carried out to the garbage can; no garbage should be spilled in the kitchen or on the way to the garbage can. The top of the garbage can should be replaced, the basket brought back into the house, a new garbage bag placed in it, and replaced under the sink.

Bedtime. You must be in bed by nine o'clock. Being in bed means that you have your pajamas on, you're under the blankets, and your head is on the pillow. At nine o'clock the light goes out and is not to be turned on again. If you are not in bed by nine o'clock on any night, you will have to go to bed one hour earlier on the following night. If on that night you are not in bed by the earlier hour, you will go to bed one hour earlier on the following night.

Cleaning your room. Your room will be clean when there are no clothes evident on the floor, under your bed, or on the furniture. All clean clothes should be hung up in the closet or replaced in drawers; all dirty clothes should be put in the dirty clothes hamper. Your bed should be made in the way that has been demonstrated to you. All papers will be picked up off the floor and from under your bed. Once a week, on Thursday afternoon, before five o'clock, you will vacuum the floor of your room. It will be approved by me or be revacuumed by you. Each day the top of your desk will be cleared and all things that are on it will be put away in drawers and the top of your desk will be cleaned and dusted. Furniture in your room will be dusted once a week and will have to pass my inspection. This dusting will occur on Wednesday afternoon and will be done before five o'clock. The daily cleaning, straightening of your room, and bed making will be done before four o'clock in the afternoon each day, and before twelve noon on Saturdays and Sundays.

Talking back. Each time that you talk back to Mom or Dad you will be sent to your room for one-half hour right at that point. It will be your responsibility to make a judgment as to what we mean by talking back, and adjust your behavior accordingly.

Arguing with siblings. If I feel that you are arguing too much and it is disturbing me or the rest of the household, I will give you a warning by saying: "If you are arguing in five minutes both of you will be sent to your room for an hour." If at the end of five minutes you are still carrying on the argument in such a way as to disturb me, you will both be sent to your room for one hour.

Weeding the garden. When you pull weeds in the garden it will be up to you, but each Saturday morning I will check the garden at ten o'clock. If it is satisfactory to me, your work is done. If it isn't satisfactory, you will continue to work in the garden until I'm satisfied that the weeds have been pulled. This may mean that you will work in the garden for several hours on Saturday, irrespective of any other plans you have.

Bedwetting. (Based on the assumption that the child has been seen by a doctor who has confirmed the absence of any organic problem.) If you wet your bed during any night, the next morning when you wake up you will take off your wet pajamas, wash them out by hand, and hang them on the line to dry. You will also change the sheets on your bed, rinsing out the sheet and depositing it in the washing machine. (This rule would mainly apply to children who are significantly older than the appropriate age for bedwetting.)

Coming home on time. You are supposed to return home from playing by five o'clock each day unless prior arrangements have been made with me about coming home later. If you are not home by five o'clock, you will not be able to watch television that night.

Consistent arguing. If you begin to argue with me when I ask or tell you to do something, you will have two minutes to state your argument. If you don't begin to do the task at the end of the two minutes, you will both do the task and be sent to your room for an hour immediately. I will determine what is excessive arguing.

X.
Limitations on the Process

The disciplinary process explained in this handbook has few limits regarding when it can be used. It has been applied to children who are border-line mentally retarded, children who have physical handicaps, and children who have minimal brain damage or some other types of organic disorders.

Where a child has severe physical disabilities, mental retardation, or other organic brain disorders, the basic principles involved in these procedures may still be used. Under such circumstances the special nature of the child must be taken into consideration when evaluating the reasonableness of the rule, the resources available to the child, the capacity of the child to perform, as well as the child's capacity to understand.

When parents are concerned about these issues, or suspect that some organic problem may be present, immediate steps should be taken to have a physical checkup done by a competent doctor who is familiar with developmental and perceptual problems of childhood. The local school district may help. It should not be assumed that a severely misbehaving child is a disabled child. Parents must definitely not attempt to make such diagnoses themselves.

XI.
There Are Some Children for Whom Rules Are Not Appropriate

Many parents object to setting up lists of rules and punishments for children. They use the justification that it would be better to reward a child for good behavior than to punish him for bad. There is ample evidence to suggest that in many cases this is true.

It has been our observation that many parents who hold this position end up feeling guilty or resentful because they have to use self-discipline to set up effective and consistent rules.

If the world were so constructed that we only received rewards for the good things we did, and the bad things were overlooked, rewarding children as a general approach would probably make more sense. Setting rules and limits for children is not only a way of managing them, but also a way of teaching them about the real world. The closer children's experiences can approach the world that they will face throughout life, the better prepared they will be to face the life in which they find themselves. It is a cruel awakening for a child who has not received punishment or had limits set for him or her in childhood to experience the reality of the adult world. Clinical observations also point out that children who have not learned to deal with limits have a very difficult time setting limits for themselves and accepting external limits when they become adults.

Notwithstanding this, there are still some occasions when it is advisable to take a "positive" approach to managing a child and to emphasize rewarding the child rather than setting up many consequences or punishments. The indications for this are fairly limited. The procedures defined in other parts of this handbook are appropriate for the overwhelming majority of children.

Here are some signs that suggest when rules and punishments will probably not work in the desired way:

- A child who has a very poor self-image and is reinforced by his own failures will need an emphasis on rewards.

- The child who is afraid to try new things, accept challenges, and has difficulty dealing with frustrating activities will probably profit from reinforcement by rewards.

- A child who is highly dependent and afraid to take on any independent tasks or work alone needs to be rewarded for any behavior which is even slightly independent.

- Brothers or sisters of a child who is highly intelligent, imaginative, independent and active may frequently find themselves being negatively compared to the "good" sibling; such a brother or sister needs rewards to feel she or he can succeed.

- The child who constantly gives evidence of having a negative self-image or excessive fears by saying such things as, "I can't do that," and "I always fail," "I'll never be able to do that," is a child who may profit from rewards.

- A child who suffers from any perceptual/motor, physical, or organic disabilities and who, because of such difficulties, experiences failure in comparison to other children of his age, needs tasks tailored to his particular needs, and to experience rewards for the accomplishment of these tasks.

All children occasionally show signs of the above characteristics. Showing some of these characteristics from time to time does not necessarily mean that the child is one of the special cases that this section talks about. Only if the child shows these signs often and to an extreme degree should he be considered a special case. In most cases, minimal evidence of these characteristics is a method for avoiding responsibility, or a way of manipulating parents to perform tasks which the children are perfectly capable of performing themselves. Only if these characteristics are clearly identified as being consistent and intense, should parents consider setting up a Star Chart as described in the following chapter.

XII.
The Star Chart

The Star Chart is an alternative to the rule list and uses the approach of rewarding the child for positive accomplishments, while minimizing punishment for bad or inappropriate behavior. Never punishing a child is probably as difficult for some parents as punishing is for others. It is also unrealistic in terms of the real world.

In setting up a Star Chart, many more areas of the child's behavior can be identified as areas for possible success experiences. The Star Chart can list as many as ten to twenty areas of possible behaviors for a child to consider. It can include a variety of different chores, provided that doing the chore is left to the child's initiative and the child is not punished for not doing them.

In other words, the child should have a number of opportunities to successfully complete chores, but should not, at the same time, be punished for not completing them. The parent need not place limitations on the number of possible chores a child can do in order to get a star on the Star Chart.

The same criteria for chores on the Star Chart should pertain as for rules. They should be reasonable; the child must have sufficient resources to accomplish them; and the child should have the capacity to do them.

In addition to listing a number of different chores on the Star Chart, the general area of behavior can have a number of items listed. These may be both "positive" and "negative" types of statements. A child may receive a star when he does not hit his brother or sister for a whole day. He may receive a star if he can get through a whole day without a tantrum or crying. Other items can include not bothering parents with unreasonable or unrealistic demands; taking care of his own physical belongings and toys. Stars can be given for successful accomplishment in school as well as for doing "nice" things for anyone in the family.

A sample Star Chart is shown in the last section of the handbook, Section 16, "Additional Material." When parents have considered the various areas in which they would like a child to begin to control his own behavior and have identified the chores which they would like the child to accomplish, they then can set up the Star Chart in the following way:

The Star Chart can be organized for a week, two weeks, or even a month-long period, depending on the age of the child and his ability to defer gratification for his successful experiences. For relatively young children, under the age of six, Star Chart reward systems should be based on short periods of time (a week). For children above the age of eight or nine, having a Star Chart that lasts for an entire month is not unreasonable in many cases. Children with really low self-esteem often cannot wait as long for their reward as those with higher self-esteem.

On a large sheet of paper or cardboard, line off columns for the individual items—chores and behaviors—for which the child can receive a star. Sufficient columns should be placed on the sheet for each day which the Star Chart is to cover. Down the left-hand side of the paper, list all of the things for which the child can receive a star. There should be one activity to a line. Along the top of the Star Chart place the child's name and the dates for which the Star Chart applies. Each of the columns should be labeled by the day and date.

Each day, when the parent sees that the child has actually accomplished one of the things on the chart, the child should have a star placed in the appropriate box. At the end of the chart period, the child should receive a reward that corresponds to previously established standards. If there are ten items for which a child can receive a reward, and there are seven days in the chart period, then the theoretical upper limit for the number of stars is seventy. The parents may wish to set the standard that if a child receives thirty stars during that period, he will receive a reward of money, some item, or be able to do something that he likes. If the child receives forty stars during that period, the reward is increased. For fifty stars, the reward is greater, etc.

Parents should have an item on the Star Chart which is not a clearly spelled out item, but nevertheless one for which the child can receive stars. This may be where the parents have the right to give an additional star for a generally good day, or a day in which the amount of misbehavior was very low. Parents should have the right to give two stars in any one box for a particularly outstanding achievement in that category.

If the child's behavior, because of emotional problems, was quite poor prior to initiating the Star Chart, the parents should be flexible in deciding what is successful completion of any item. As time goes on and the child develops more confidence and ability to perform chores, the standards for successfully performing one of the activities should rise.

XIII.
Rewards for Star Chart Performance

If parents use this approach, the obvious question is what kind of reward should be given to the child for successful performance? The giving of rewards generally follows the same principles as punishments. Rewards should be based on what the child values or finds important.

Praise, encouragement, smiles, and applause are rewards, and should be used in addition to tangible concrete rewards such as:

- Money.

- Toys or games for which the child has asked.

- Activities the child enjoys doing or has indicated he would like to do, like boardwalks, funhouses, etc.

Which type of reward or combinations of types to use depends on the values of the family. In a family in which money is important, the children in the family will usually adopt it as an important criterion of their success. Parents should not confuse the use of monetary rewards with the problem of bribes. If it has already been determined that the child is in need of a reward system, and money is valued in the family, then it should be used as a reward for accomplishment. Most of us get paid for the work we do, even if we also profit from doing it in non-material ways.

Using the previous example of the ten-item, seven-day Star Chart, in which it is possible to accumulate seventy stars, parents should grade the system so that twenty stars at the end of one week should be worth a quarter, thirty stars at the end of the week worth fifty cents, forty stars worth seventy-five cents, etc., or any other monetary reward that the parents determine. The main caution is to be careful not to set up a system that will break the bank. Also, the child should not receive such large amounts of money that this in itself becomes a problem.

If material rewards are used, then they can also be graded. If a child receives twenty stars, he receives a reward worth a quarter to fifty cents. If he receives forty stars, he receives a reward that may be worth one dollar, etc.

If activities are used as a reward, then parents must be very careful to honor promises regarding the time and place at which the reward is to be given. They should take care to insure that any promised reward can be fulfilled as soon as possible after the completion of the Star Chart. If the Star Chart lasts from Monday to Monday, and the only time that the parents can provide the activity reward is on the following weekend, this would delay the receipt of the reward for almost a week. Younger children might find this time lag uncomfortable.

If the parents promise an activity which takes place outdoors during a time of the year when the weather is unpredictable, they run the risk of not being able to fulfill the reward because of conditions outside their control. Young children might experience a good deal of frustration and resentment if this were to happen. They might feel that their accomplishment was not being honored by the parent, and this may lead to argument and bad feeling. Parents who wish to avoid this should be sure they do have a reasonable chance of fulfilling whatever promised reward they made to the child.

In order to keep from giving too much money when a child does extremely well on the Star Chart, as an example, getting sixty out of seventy possible stars, rewards could be combinations of the three types indicated above. In other words, if a child does extremely well, he may get a little money, a gift of some material object, plus some valued activity.

The major point to keep in mind in all of this is that the rewards must be consistent with the things that the child and the family consider important, and most especially that the *child* must find the rewards to be of value.

XIV.
Adolescents

Will the rule setting as described in this handbook work for teenagers?

The basic approach can work with all children and, in fact, all people. Adolescents are no less in need of having a secure home life than are young children. Their capacity to tolerate situations that are unclear rises somewhat, but nevertheless, many adolescents are still confused about what their parents want from them—what the expectations are, and what the standards are for performance.

Because of physical size and social experience, adolescents have a number of additional tools to use in their conflicts with parents. But the need to organize a family system where adolescents are present is not diminished. On the contrary, because of increased mobility, growth in the teenagers' capacity to make decisions for himself, etc., family disfunction can become more extreme during adolescence, and greater order and discipline are definitely required.

The process described in this handbook can be used with adolescents, but the important qualification is that the adolescent himself must become more involved in the process. The teenager must be able to discuss with the parent the problems and the requirements. Also, the issue of consequences for breaking rules is somewhat different for teenagers than it is for younger children.

Most teenagers will accept the reality of having consequences for their behavior. Possibly the one exception to the success of this approach with teenagers lies in its application to juvenile delinquents. Here, by definition, is a situation in which a child has lived for most of his life without a clear system of rules in the home. Therefore, the application of this procedure to children who are clearly delinquent is difficult. Where younger children live in the home, this process can still be applied for clarifying situations and creating more order in the home, thus perhaps indirectly influencing the delinquent teenager.

Teenagers will require more flexibility in the time required for completion of tasks, but in order to make work meaningful for them there should be a substantial degree of obligation in the household. It is more difficult to control the relationship between teenagers and their parents. Parents of adolescents are forced to look at themselves a lot more critically because teenagers' criticisms and observations of the parents and their behavior are frequently accurate. Parents of teenagers must be willing to discuss things with their teenagers, especially when the teenager feels things need to be discussed.

Order and discipline in the home are still important factors in the life of teenagers. It is interesting that informal observation of delinquent teenagers has indicated that in *almost all* cases the parents were unable to indicate any consistent rules and responsibilities which were required of the delinquent as a child. Family problems may be seen as one of the causes of delinquency, but the basic cause of family problems seems to be the absence of specific rules, limits, and predictable consequences for the child's behavior. Teenagers who are not labeled as delinquents, but who may be experiencing problems which are easily resolved by brief therapy, have all been raised, to some degree, in a family with rules and order.

Lack of predictability and confusion in family communications produces excessive anxiety in a child or adolescent. This anxiety must be dealt with. The process described in this manual is not only for children, but will also create security, and higher self-esteem in all family members. When parents are secure, their children automatically become more secure. Through this security the child feels less of the internal pressure that causes him to express feelings in inappropriate ways, and there is a greater opportunity for more normal and natural relationships between parents and children. It also provides the parent with the security and self-esteem to listen to the child more effectively.

XV.
Teaching the Child to Be Responsible

The motive for having children follow rules is to teach them to assume responsibility. When a child is given the responsibility for taking out the garbage, and he needs to be constantly reminded by the parent, the parent still has the responsibility for seeing that the garbage is taken out, and the child is acting as the parent's agent. Thus, when the parent does not remind the child, the job is not done.

Setting rules and consequences in the manner described in this manual is a way of encouraging the child to take responsibilities. When a child knows that he has a job, and if it is not performed, certain consequences follow, that child will be encouraged to take his responsibilities more seriously.

Teaching responsibility is reality-training for the child. Inappropriate behavior by children may be viewed as signs that they are not taking responsibility for their own behavior. When a child continually needs to be reprimanded for something he's doing, it shows that the child is not taking responsibility *himself* for that behavior. When children do not learn in school, it usually shows that they are not taking responsibility for learning or that the teacher is robbing them of responsibility. Parents rob children when they assume responsibility for the child's behavior. Reminders, prodding, doing it instead of the child doing it—are ways in which parents take responsibility away from the child.

Training in responsibility-taking is one of the chief contributions parents can make to the development of children. When a child knows what to do, and when to do it, the responsibility for completing that task should be the child's.

When parents are not responsible for performing their duties as parents in an effective and disciplined way, they cannot assume that a child will be any more responsible in carrying out his tasks. Parents who are irresponsible do not provide a model for responsibility-taking in their children. **Undisciplined parents have undisciplined children.**

Setting appropriate rules is a way of training children in responsibility. Simply punishing them for not doing right may control their actions, but does not effectively train them in responsibility-taking.

When a child begins to take responsibility in some area of his life, it will affect other areas. We have witnessed, over and over again, that when a child is subjected to rules and consequences at home, he begins to take more responsibility than that defined by the rules. In many cases, the child's behavior in school, where no interventions were made, also changes significantly.

Taking responsibility builds self-esteem, and higher self-esteem will affect all areas of a child's life.

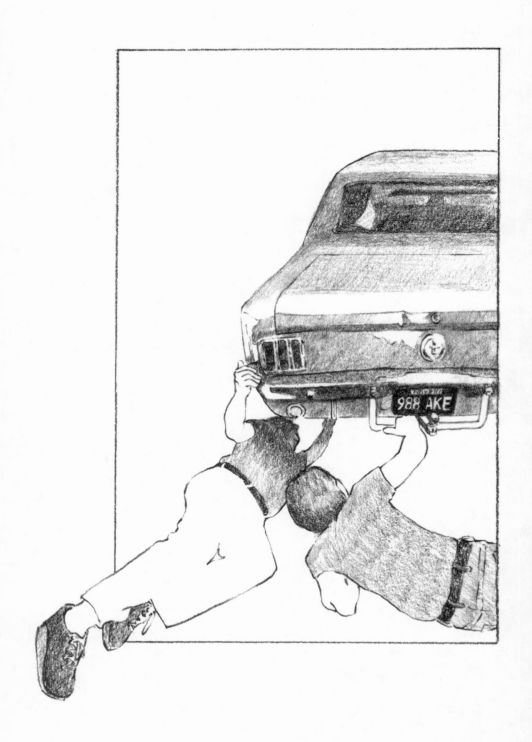

XVI.
Additional Materials

A. Questions to Ask Yourself When Analyzing a Problem:

1. When does our child do this?

2. How do I react when he does it?

3. Can I remember a time when I didn't react that way?

   a) How did our child respond to my reaction?
   b) How did I feel about what I did?

4. Can I remember a time when, in spite of the usual conditions being present, our child did not act this way?

   a) What, if anything, was different?
   b) Do I understand why this happened?
   c) Is it possible to recreate those conditions?

5. How will I react if my child does this?

6. What stops me from reacting this way?

7. What can help or encourage me to react the way I would like?

8. How would I like our child to act?

9. Does he do this only when I'm around?

10. Do other people tell me about it, or can I observe it directly?

11. Is there any way in which I can see that I actually encourage my child to act this way?

12. Have I ever talked to him about this?

    a) What did he say about it?
    b) Did I understand him?

13. Does my spouse react the same way I do?

    a) If not, what is the difference?
    b) How do these different reactions affect our child?
    c) Is there some way we can agree to react?

B. A Sample Star Chart:

STAR CHART

For: Amy Brown   Sept. 21–Sept. 27,

THINGS TO WORK AT:	SAT. Sept. 21	SUN. Sept. 22	MON. Sept. 23	TUE. Sept. 24	WED. Sept. 25	THUR. Sept. 26	FRI. Sept. 27
1. Pick up your toys							
2. Feed the dog							
3. Don't hit your little brother							
4. Come home on time							
5. Make your bed							
6. Brush your teeth							
7. Don't cry							
8. Bring school papers home							
9. Be nice all day							
10. Don't bother Mom when she is busy							
11. Go to bed on time							
12. Don't make a fuss at dinner							
13. Do 2 things you are asked to do							
14.							
15.							
16.							
17.							

C. The Problems I'm Having with My Child: A Checklist

Look at this list—it might surprise you. Parents sometimes "solve" a problem behavior by seeing it as "something the child will outgrow," which results in the parent tolerating the behavior. This often only perpetuates the problem. Parents *can* get used to anything; but they don't have to.

At some time, all children do most of the behaviors listed below. A problem exists when a child repeats the behavior habitually, and parents can't seem to stop it.

_____ Talks back to parents or other adults

_____ Won't go to bed on time

_____ Keeps room too messy

_____ Repeatedly hits siblings or other children

_____ Wets the bed

_____ Pouts most of the time

_____ Whines when asked to do things

_____ Eats improperly at the table

_____ Won't do assigned chores

_____ Argues when told to do something

_____ Forgets when told to do something

_____ Lies

_____ Cries when he doesn't get his way

_____ Tries to avoid going to school

_____ Plays with matches and sets fires

_____ Teases pets

_____ Doesn't come home on time

_____ Doesn't pick up after self

_____ Steals

_____ Won't pay attention when told to do something

_____ Starts fights or arguments with others

_____ Won't play with other children

_____ Always telling others what to do

_____ Makes too much noise

_____ Won't get out of bed on time

_____ Breaks toys and other objects

D. Chores Your Child Can Do: Reference List

Key:
   ❖❖❖ Children at these ages *may* be able to perform chore
   _ _ _ Children at these ages *should* be able to perform chore

Ages at which chore can be done:

Chore	2	3	4	5	6	7	8	9	10	11	12
1. Wash dishes				❖	❖	❖	❖	❖	–	–	–
2. Pick up belongings (toys, clothes)	❖	–	–	–	–	–	–	–	–	–	–
3. Clean room, minimally				❖	❖	❖	–	–	–	–	–
4. Clean room, expertly					❖	❖	❖	❖			
5. Feed pets			❖	❖	–	–	–	–	–	–	–
6. Mow the lawn							❖	❖	–	–	–
7. Wash the bathtub				❖	❖	❖	–	–	–	–	–
8. Take out the garbage				❖	❖	❖	❖	–	–	–	–
9. Sweep the patio or porch				❖	❖	❖	–	–	–	–	–
10. Put toys away	❖	❖	–	–	–	–	–	–	–	–	–
11. Clean the garage						❖	❖	❖	–	–	–
12. Vacuum					❖	❖	❖	❖	–	–	–
13. Clean the bathroom				❖	❖	❖	–	–	–	–	–
14. Wash clothes using washing machine						❖	❖	❖	–	–	–
15. Set the table				❖	❖	–	–	–	–	–	–

Note: The age provisions on this chart apply to most children. If your child is special, because of a physical or mental handicap, you should seek professional advice regarding the best time to implement chores. Children vary in the timing of their development, and you need to consider those things your child can do comfortably. There aren't any "good" or "bad" chores; it's most important that your child be expected to do *something*.

Ages at which chore can be done:

	2	3	4	5	6	7	8	9	10	11	12
16. Clear the table				◆	◆	◆	-	-	-	-	-
17. Pull weeds					◆	◆	-	-	-	-	-
18. Dust furniture, minimally				◆	◆	◆	-	-	-	-	-
19. Dust furniture, expertly						◆	◆	-	-	-	-
20. Make bed					◆	◆	◆	-	-	-	-
21. Help mother or father with a variety of chores	-	-	-	-	-	-	-	-	-	-	-
22. Baby-sit younger siblings for brief periods									◆	-	-
23. Cook meals								◆	◆	-	-
24. Make lunch for school					◆	◆	-	-	-	-	-
25. Wash windows (if easily reached)								◆	-	-	-
26. Wash the car							◆	◆	-	-	-
27. Sweep floors							◆	◆	-	-	-
28. Work in vegetable garden				◆	◆	-	-	-	-	-	-
29. Water house plants					◆	◆	-	-	-	-	-
30. Clean pet feeding area				◆	◆	-	-	-	-	-	-

Chores Your Child Can Do

Chores Your Child Can Do

NEW

TEACHER/PARENT RESOURCE BOOKS

• DISCIPLINE • RESPONSIBILITY • SELF-ESTEEM

These Resource Books offer practical techniques for dealing with children who have learning and/or behavioral problems. The books are written in an easy to understand, straight-forward style. They offer sound advice from family counselors in the areas that are most important to improving children's school performance.

Reynold Bean, Ed.M.   Harris Clemes, Ph.D.

HOW TO RAISE CHILDREN'S SELF-ESTEEM
This handbook shows how to help children improve: Self-confidence–Values and attitudes–Interaction with others.

HOW TO RAISE TEENAGERS' SELF-ESTEEM
Case examples illustrate: New approaches to teenager problems–Analyses of self-esteem problems–Guides to raising self-esteem.

HOW TO DISCIPLINE CHILDREN WITHOUT FEELING GUILTY
Adults can learn to direct children effectively by: Rewarding good behavior–Fitting chores to the child–Being consistent with discipline.

HOW TO TEACH CHILDREN RESPONSIBILITY
This handbook defines responsibility and provides practical activities for teaching responsibility: Helps children solve problems in school and at home.